Golda

This book belongs to:

About Ysolda

Ysolda Teague is a young Scottish designer who has published popular designs in Twist Collective and knitty. This is the second book in a series, the first along with her many other patterns can be found on her website and blog, ysolda.com and on ravelry.com. Ysolda lives and works in Edinburgh but loves to travel, especially when it means meeting the people who make her patterns.

Thank you!

to Sheena Stewart, Struan Teague, Sarah Stanfield, Hannah Haworth, Alison Green Will and Gudrun Johnston for all of your help in putting together this collection; to Laura Chau for her skillful tech editing and endless patience with my pestering; to all of the yarn companies who so generously provided the beautiful yarns used in these patterns; to Jessica Marshall Forbes, Casey Forbes, Mary-Heather Cogar and Sarah Bible for everything that is Ravelry; and most of all thank you to all of the knitters who've knit my patterns and supported me in so many very unexpected and wonderful ways.

Confused?

If you're not sure how to do something or are confused by an instruction have a look at the support page on my website which has links to many useful tutorials and answers to frequently asked questions.
http://ysolda.com/support/
If that doesn't help you can email me at support@ysolda.com

Published by Ysolda Teague © Ysolda Teague 2009

Whimsical Little Knits

2

by Golda

Abbreviations

k - knit

p - purl

st(s) - stitch(es)

st st - stockinette / stocking st

bo - bind off, also known as cast off

sl - slip, slip all sts purlwise with yarn at back except when working a decrease

w+t - with yarn at front sl1, bring yarn to back, return sl st to left needle, turn (if next st is a k bring yarn to back)

pm - place marker

slm - slip marker

k2tog - knit 2 together

ssk - slip, slip, knit slipped sts together

p2tog - purl 2 together

sl1, k2tog, psso - slip 1, k2tog, lift sl st over st just worked

k3tog - knit 3 together

kfb - k in front and back of next st

yo - yarn over

m1(p) - make one (pick up the strand between the needles from the front and place on the left needle tip, knit or purl it through the back loop)

RLI - k into the st immediately below the next st

LLI - k into the st 2 rows below the previous st

inc 4 - (k1, p1)twice, k1 into next st

beg - begin(ning)

rnd(s) - round(s)

rep(s) - repeat(s)

rem - remaining

dpn(s) - double pointed needle(s)

circ - circular needle

RS - right side

WS - wrong side

MC - main colour

CC - contrast colour

T2B - sl1 st to cable needle and hold at back, k1, p1 st from cable needle

T2F - sl1 st to cable needle and hold at front, p1, k1 st from cable needle

T3B - sl1 st to cable needle and hold at back, k2, p1 st from cable needle

T3F - sl2 sts to cable needle and hold at front, p1, k2 sts from cable needle

T4B - sl2 sts to cable needle and hold at back, k2, p2 sts from cable needle

T4F - sl2 sts to cable needle and hold at front, p2, k2 sts from cable needle

C2B - sl1 st to cable needle and hold at back, k1, k1 st from cable needle

C2F - sl1 st to cable needle and hold at front, k1, k1 st from cable needle.

C4B - sl2 sts to cable needle and hold at back, k2, k2 sts from cable needle

C4F - sl2 sts to cable needle and hold at front, k2, k2 sts from cable needle

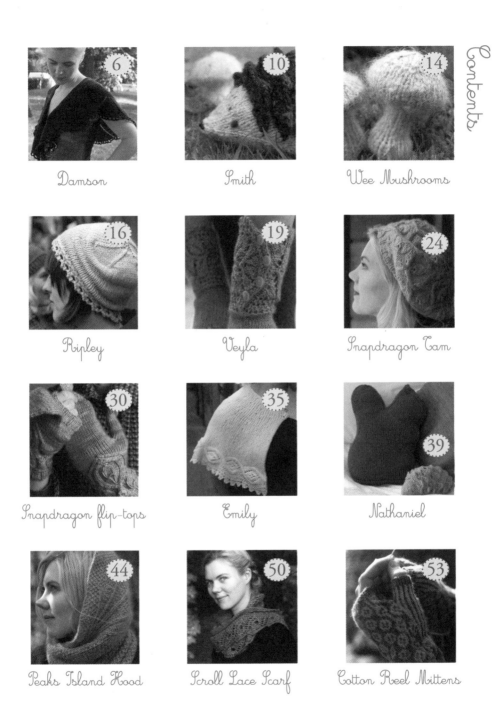

Damson

A pretty, simple little shawl, requiring just one skein of sock yarn, that's fun to knit and easy to wear. Working two columns of paired yarn over increases that radiate from the centre neck cast on creates a curved shape that drapes perfectly around your shoulders. Increasing at the edges on both right and wrong side rows results in long points that make Damson ideal to wear as a scarf. Large scale lace creates a dramatic scalloped edge, finished with a deceptively simple looped edging.

Materials

440 yds / 402m fingering (4ply) weight yarn.
Shown in Malabrigo Sock (100% merino, 440 yds / 402 m, 3.53oz /100g) in Eggplant.
Size 6 US / 4mm circular needle (24" / 60cm or longer)

Gauge

24 sts and 34 rows = 4" / 10cm in st st

Size

Approx 22" / 56cm from centre to point and 12" / 30cm from centre to bottom edge.

Notes

Refer to table on p.9 for stitch counts at the end of each row. Where no count is given it remains unchanged.

Directions

Cast on 3 sts; knit 6 rows. Pick up and k 3 sts from vertical edge of garter stitch, then 3 sts from cast on edge. 9 sts.

Garter st section

Row 1 (WS): k to end.

Row 2: k3, (yo, k1) 3 times, yo, k3.

Row 3: k3, yo, k to 3 sts from end, yo, k3.

Row 4: k3, yo, k3, (yo, pm, k1, yo, k1) twice, k2, yo, k3.

Row 5: k3, yo, k to 3 sts from end, yo, k3.

Row 6: k3, yo, (k to marker, yo, slm, k1, yo) twice, k to 3 sts from end, yo, k3.

Rows 7-72: rep rows 5 and 6 33 more times.

Lace section

Remove markers as you come to them on next row.

Row 73: k3, yo, p to 3 sts from end, yo, k3.

Row 74 and all following right side rows: work scallop lace pattern from written or charted directions below.

Row 75 and all following wrong side rows: k3, p to 3 sts from end, k3.

Scallop lace pattern - written directions

Row 74: k3, yo, (k1, yo, k16, sl1, k2tog, psso, k16, yo) 8 times, k1, yo, k3.

Row 76: k3, yo, (k3, yo, k15, sl1, k2tog, psso, k15, yo) 8 times, k3, yo, k3.

Row 78: k3, yo, (k5, yo, k14, sl1, k2tog, psso, k14, yo) 8 times, k5, yo, k3.

Row 80: k3, yo, (k7, yo, k13, sl1, k2tog, psso, k13, yo) 8 times, k7, yo, k3.

Row 82: k3, yo, (k9, yo, k12, sl1, k2tog, psso, k12, yo) 8 times, k9, yo, k3.

Row 84: k3, yo, (k11, yo, k11, sl1, k2tog, psso, k11, yo) 8 times, k11, yo, k3.

Row 86: k3, yo, (k13, yo, k10, sl1, k2tog, psso, k10, yo) 8 times, k13, yo, k3.

Row 88: k3, yo, (k15, yo, k9, sl1, k2tog, psso, k9, yo) 8 times, k15, yo, k3.

Row 90: k3, yo, (k17, yo, k8, sl1, k2tog, psso, k8, yo) 8 times, k17, yo, k3.

Row 92: k3, yo, (k19, yo, k7, sl1, k2tog, psso, k7, yo) 8 times, k19, yo, k3.

Row 94: k3, yo, (k21, yo, k6, sl1, k2tog, psso, k6, yo) 8 times, k21, yo, k3.

Row 96: k3, yo, (k23, yo, k5, sl1, k2tog, psso, k5, yo) 8 times, k23, yo, k3.

1. co 3 sts
2. k 6 rows
3. pick up sts

22" / 56cm

12" / 31cm

Damson

Row 98: k3, yo, (k25, yo, k4, sl1, k2tog, psso, k4, yo) 8 times, k25, yo, k3.

Row 100: k3, yo, (k27, yo, k3, sl1, k2tog, psso, k3, yo) 8 times, k27, yo, k3.

Row 102: k3, yo, (k29, yo, k2, sl1, k2tog, psso, k2, yo) 8 times, k29, yo, k3.

Row 104: k3, yo, (k31, yo, k1, sl1, k2tog, psso, k1, yo) 8 times, k31, yo, k3.

Row 106: k3, yo, (k33, yo, sl1, k2tog, psso, yo) 8 times, k33, yo, k3.

Edging

Row 107: k to end.

Row 108: k4, (yo twice, sl1, k2tog, psso) to 4 sts from end, yo twice, k4.

Row 109: k4, *(k1, p1) twice into double yo, k1, rep from * to 3 sts from end, k3.

Bind off.

8

Finishing

Weave in ends and block to the shape shown in schematic, stretching loops of edging open and pinning. Measurements given are an approximate guide, focus on opening up the lace rather than achieving the exact size.

Stitch counts the number of sts between the markers in the garter stitch section on right side rows equals the number of the row.

row	sts	row	sts	row	sts
1	9	32	133	63	255
2	13	33	135	64	261
3	15	34	141	65	263
4	21	35	143	66	269
5	23	36	149	67	271
6	29	37	151	68	277
7	31	38	157	69	279
8	37	39	159	70	285
9	39	40	165	71	287
10	45	41	167	72	293
11	47	42	173	73	295
12	53	43	175	74	297
13	55	44	181	76	299
14	61	45	183	78	301
15	63	46	189	80	303
16	69	47	191	82	305
17	71	48	197	84	307
18	77	49	199	86	309
19	79	50	205	88	311
20	85	51	207	90	313
21	87	52	213	92	315
22	93	53	215	94	317
23	95	54	221	96	319
24	101	55	223	98	321
25	103	56	229	100	323
26	109	57	231	102	325
27	111	58	237	104	327
28	117	59	239	106	329
29	119	60	245	108	331
30	125	61	247	109	547
31	127	62	253		

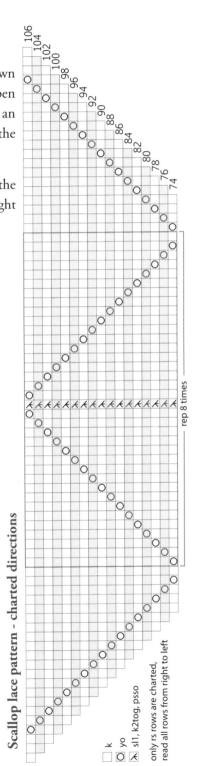

Scallop lace pattern - charted directions

rep 8 times

☐ k
◯ yo
⋏ sl1, k2tog, psso

only rs rows are charted,
read all rows from right to left

Smith

is an adorable Hedgehog that can be knit in a variety of sizes by using different yarn weights. Although knitting anything with spikes is going to be a little fiddly, the construction method used is simple and fun. The body is worked in the round and the spikes are worked in separate pieces and joined to the body as you go, this also makes it easy to work the spikes in a darker colour if desired. Smith was inspired by one of my favourite childhood books, *Smith the Lonely Hedgehog* by Althea.

In addition to the yarn and needles detailed opposite you will also need toy stuffing.

Notes

Optional: work the spikes in contrast colour.

If using a single colour, wind yarn into a centre pull ball and work body from centre and spikes from outside.

Directions

With smaller needles cast on 6 sts using the method detailed here: http://techknitting.blogspot.com/2007/02/casting-on-from-middle-disappearing.html
Distribute sts evenly onto 3 needles and knit 1 rnd.

Body section 1
Rnd 2: kfb in each stitch. 12 sts.
Rnd 3: k.
Rnd 4: (k1, kfb) to end. 18 sts.
Rnd 5: k.

Rnd 6: (k2, kfb) to end. 24 sts.
Rnd 7: k.
Rnd 8: (k3, kfb) to end. 30 sts.
Put aside but do not break yarn.

1st row of spikes
With larger needles and 2nd ball of yarn cast on 17sts.
Row 1: k2tog, k1, kfb twice, k2, k3tog, k1, kfb twice, k2, k2tog; rep row 1 3 more times; break yarn.

Joining spikes and body

Using illustration as a guide hold spikes in front of body so that the 2 needles are parallel and work **rnd 9:** k1 body st, then k 1 spike st tog with 1 body st until all spike sts are joined; k to end of rnd.

	Big Smith	Little Smith	Teeny, tiny Smith
Yarn for solid coloured version	130yds / 120m heavy worsted (aran) weight yarn. Shown in Blue Sky Alpacas Organic Cotton (100% cotton, 150 yds / 102 m, 3.53oz /100g) in Nut.	100yds / 90m double knitting weight yarn.	80yds / 75m fingering (4ply) weight yarn.
Yarn for body	65yds / 60m heavy worsted (aran) weight yarn.	50yds / 45m double knitting weight yarn. Shown in Rowan Scottish Tweed DK (100% wool, 123 yds / 112 m, 1.76oz / 50g) in Oatmeal.	40yds / 37m fingering (4ply) weight yarn. Shown in British Alpaca 4ply in light brown.
Yarn for spikes	65yds / 60m heavy worsted (aran) weight yarn.	50yds / 45m double knitting weight yarn. Shown in Rowan Scottish Tweed DK in Peat.	40yds / 37m fingering (4ply) weight yarn. Shown in British Alpaca 4ply in dark brown.
Needles for body	Size 7 US / 4.5mm dpns	Size 2.5 US / 3mm dpns	Size 0 US / 2mm dpns
Needles for spikes	Size 9 US / 5.5mm straights	Size 6 US / 4mm straights	Size 2.5 US / 3mm straights
Gauge for body	18 sts = 4" / 10cm in st st	24 sts = 4" / 10cm in st st	36 sts = 4" / 10cm in st st
Length	9" / 23cm	6" / 15cm	4" / 10cm

Body section 2

Rnd 10: (k4, kfb) to end. 36 sts.

Rnd 11: k.

Rnd 12: (k5, kfb) to end. 42 sts.

2nd row of spikes

With larger needles and 2nd ball of yarn cast on 25sts.

Row 1: k2tog, k1, (kfb twice, k2, k3tog, k1) twice, kfb twice, k2, k2tog; rep row 1 3 more times; break yarn.

Body section 3

Rnd 13: rep rnd 9 to join spike and body sts.

Rnd 14: (k6, kfb) to end. 48 sts.

Rnd 15: k.

Rnd 16: (k7, kfb) to end. 54 sts.

3rd row of spikes

With larger needles and 2nd ball of yarn cast on 33sts.

Row 1: k2tog, k1, (kfb twice, k2, k3tog, k1) 3 times, kfb twice, k2, k2tog; rep row 1 3 more times; break yarn.

Body section 4

Rnd 17: rep rnd 9 to join spike and body sts.

Rnd 18: (k8, kfb) 4 times, k to end. 58 sts.

Rnd 19: k.

Rnd 20: (k9, kfb) 4 times, k to end. 62 sts.

4th row of spikes

With larger needles and 2nd ball of yarn cast on 41sts.

Row 1: k2tog, k1, (kfb twice, k2, k3tog, k1) 4 times, kfb twice, k2, k2tog; rep row 1 3 more times; break yarn.

Body section 5

Rnd 21: rep rnd 9 to join spike and body sts.

Rnds 22-24: k 3 rnds.

5th row of spikes

With larger needles and 2nd ball of yarn cast on 41sts.

Row 1: kfb, k2, k3tog, k1, (kfb twice, k2, k3tog, k1) 4 times, kfb, k1; rep row 1 3 more times; break yarn.

Body section 6

Rnd 25: rep rnd 9 to join spike and body sts.

Rnds 26-28: k 3 rnds.

6th, 7th and 8th rows of spikes and body sections 7 and 8

Work 4th row of spikes, body section 5, 5th row of spikes and body section 6 once more; then work 4th row of spikes once again.

Body section 9

Rnd 37: rep rnd 9 to join spike and body sts.

Rnd 38: (k9, k2tog) 4 times, k to end. 58 sts.

Rnd 39: k.
Rnd 40: (k8, k2tog) 4 times, k to end. 54 sts.

9th row of spikes Work as for 3rd row of spikes.

Body section 10
Rnd 41: rep rnd 9 to join spike and body sts.
Rnd 42: (k7, k2tog) to end. 48 sts.
Rnd 43: k.
Rnd 44: (k6, k2tog) to end. 42 sts.

10th row of spikes
With larger needles and 2nd ball of yarn cast on 25sts.
Row 1: kfb, k2, k3tog, k1, (kfb twice, k2, k3tog, k1) twice, kfb, k1; rep row 1 3 more times; break yarn.

Head
Stuff body to within a few rnds of the needles, continue to add small amounts of stuffing to the head after every few rnds have been worked.
Rnd 45: rep rnd 9 to join spike and body sts.
Rnd 46: (k5, k2tog) to end. 36 sts.
Rnd 47-48: k 2 rnds.
Rnd 49: (k4, k2tog) to end. 30 sts.
Rnd 50-51: k 2 rnds.
Rnd 52: (k3, k2tog) to end. 24 sts.
Rnd 53-54: k 2 rnds.
Rnd 55: (k2, k2tog) to end. 18 sts.
Rnd 56-57: k 2 rnds.
Rnd 58: (k1, k2tog) to end. 12 sts.
Rnd 59-60: k 2 rnds.
Finish stuffing the head.
Rnd 61: (k2tog) to end. 6 sts.
Break yarn and draw through remaining sts, pull up tightly and bury end securely on the inside.

Finishing
Bury remaining ends securely on the inside. Embroider french knot eyes.

Wee mushrooms

Sweet little mushrooms weighted with coins so that they can stand up on their own. Make them to go with Smith the hedgehog, or just as a decoration.

Materials

Small amount of double knitting weight yarn in two colours. Shown in Rowan Scottish Tweed DK in Oatmeal and Porridge.

3mm dpns; toy stuffing; 4 pennies or other coins approx 3/4" / 2cm in diameter.

Size

The finished size can easily be varied but the mushrooms pictured are approx 2.5" / 7cm tall.

Directions

Cast on 6 sts using the method detailed here: http://techknitting. blogspot.com/2007/02/casting-on-from-middle-disappearing.html

Distribute sts evenly onto 3 needles and knit 1 rnd.

A safety pin can be used to mark the end of the rnd.

Rnd 2: kfb in each stitch. 12 sts.
K 12 - 20 rnds depending on how tall you want the stalk to be.
Next rnd: (k1, kfb) to end. 18 sts.
Next rnd: (k2, kfb) to end. 24 sts.
Next rnd: (k3, kfb) to end. 30 sts.
Next rnd: (k4, kfb) to end. 36 sts.

Vary the size of the cap by varying the number of increase rounds working in this manner. Remember to also change the corresponding decrease rounds in the same way.

Switch to contrast colour for cap and k 8 rnds.

Next rnd: (k4, k2tog) to end. 30 sts.
Next rnd: k.
Next rnd: (k3, k2tog) to end. 24 sts.
Stack 4 pennies at base of stalk, then stuff to within a couple of rnds of needles.
Next rnd: k.
Next rnd: (k2, k2tog) to end. 18 sts.
Next rnd: k.
Next rnd: (k1, k2tog) to end. 12 sts.
Next rnd: k2tog to end. 6 sts.
Finish stuffing cap; break yarn and draw through rem sts pulling up tightly and burying the end on the inside.

Ripley

A fun, versatile hat with a couple of simple variations on the basic pattern that lead to a completely different style. Sculptural pleats can be worn at the side for a cute vintage style cloche with a girly lace edge. Shown at the back of the slouchier version they help all of that extra fabric drape perfectly, the casual slouchiness and neat garter stitch band result in a more modern, unisex look. Of course if you happen to want a slouchy hat with a lace edging you can combine the different elements however you like.

Materials

Less slouchy version - 72[80, 88, 96]yds / 66[73, 81, 88]m; slouchy version - 96[108, 118, 130]yds / 89[98, 108, 118]m heavy worsted / aran weight yarn. Shown in Blue Sky Alpacas Worsted Hand Dyes (50% alpaca / 50% merino, 100 yds / 91m, 3.53oz /100g) in charcoal and light blue.

Size 10 US / 6mm 16" / 40cm circular; Size 10 US / 6mm dpns; 1 dpn in a smaller size; 6 markers; waste yarn for holding sts.

Gauge 14 sts and 22 rnds = 4" / 10cm in st st

Sizes xs[s, m, l] to fit head circumference of 18[20, 22, 24]" / 46[51, 56, 61]cm.

Directions

Begin by working either the lace or plain band. Band is worked back and forth in rows on 2 larger dpns.

Lace band

Provisionally cast on 5 sts.

Row 1: k4, p1.

Row 2: sl1, k4.

Row 3: bind off 2, k2 (including st left on right needle after bind off), p1.

Row 4: sl1, k1, yo twice, k1.

Row 5: k1, (k1, p1) into double yo, k1, p1.

Rep rows 2-5 17[19, 21, 23] more times, 36[40, 44, 48] slipped sts.

Break yarn and slip sts onto scrap yarn.

Plain band

Provisionally cast on 7 sts.

Row 1: k6, p1.

Row 2: sl1, k5, p1.

Rep row 2 71[79, 87, 95] more times, 36[40, 44, 48] slipped sts on each side. Break yarn and slip sts onto scrap yarn.

Picking up sts from the band - both versions

Using circular needle, with WS facing and starting at the end just worked pick up and knit sts along long straight edge of band. Pick up sts by inserting left needle tip from front to back under both strands of slipped st and k these strands together as though they were a normal st; continue in this way, working from right to left until all slipped sts have been used. 36[40, 44, 48] sts.

Hat

Without joining in the rnd turn.

Next row: (k1, kfb) to end. 54[60, 66, 72] sts.

Join rnd, placing marker to mark beginning of rnd.

Pleats

K 10 rnds.

Next rnd: k10, work pleat over 14 sts as follows:

working from the wrong side use smaller dpn to pick up the top loops of the sts 8 rnds below the next 14 sts.

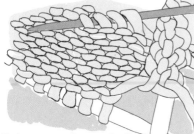

Slide sts to other end of dpn.

Hold left tip of circ and dpn parallel and use right tip to knit each st on dpn tog with a st on the circ; when all sts from dpn have been used, k to end of rnd.

K 10 rnds.

Next rnd: k11, work 2nd pleat in the same way as first over next 12 sts, k to end of rnd.

K 10 rnds.

Next rnd: k12, work 3rd pleat over next 10 sts, k to end of rnd.

For less slouchy hat: k1 rnd; proceed to crown decrease section.

For slouchier hat: k10 rnds; proceed to crown decrease section.

Crown decreases

Next rnd: (k9[10, 11, 12], pm) to end.

Next rnd: (k to 2 sts before marker, k2tog, slm) to end.

Next rnd: k.

Next rnd: (k to 2 sts before marker, k2tog, slm) to end.

Switching to dpns when there are too few sts to comfortably fit on circular rep last rnd until 12 sts remain, k2tog around.

Finishing

Break yarn and draw through 6 rem sts, pull up tightly and weave in tail on wrong side.

Remove waste yarn from band sts and slip each set onto dpns. Kitchener st the ends of the band together.

Weave in ends.

Veyla

Pretty fingerless mitts with a buttoned lace cuff. The cuff, featuring a drooping elm leaf pattern, is worked back and forth and then stitches are picked up along one edge and the rest of the mitt is knit in the round downwards. Thumb increases and a single leaf motif on the back of the hand echo the lace cuff. Requiring just a small amount of fingering weight yarn, Veyla are the perfect way to use a special, luxury yarn.

19

Materials

160[185]yds / 147[170]m fingering (4ply) weight yarn. Shown in The Fibre Company Canopy Fingering (50% alpaca, 30% merino, 20% bamboo, 200 yds / 183 m, 1.76oz /50g) in Blue Crown.

Size 3 US / 3.25mm dpns or circular(s) for your preferred method of working small diameters in the round.

8 small buttons, approx .4" / 1cm in diameter.

Gauge

28 sts and 36 rnds = 4" / 10cm in st st

Sizes

s[l] to fit approx measurement around knuckles of 7.5[8.5]" / 19[22]cm and 8.5[9]" / 22[23] cm long.

Directions

Right cuff

Cast on 23 sts.

Row 1 (WS): k to 1 st from end, p1.

Row 2: sl1, (k3, yo, k2tog) 4 times, k2.

Row 3: k1 to 1 st from end, p1.

Row 4: sl1, k to end.

Working from chart or written directions below work row 1 of right cuff lace pattern, then work rows 2-9 6[7]times.

Next row (RS): sl1, k to end.

Next row: k to 1 st from end, p1.

Rep last 2 rows once; bind off.

Right cuff lace pattern - written directions

Row 1 (WS): k2, p4, k1, p7, k1, p4, k3, p1.

Row 2: sl1, k2tog, (yo, k1) 3 times, ssk, p1, k2tog, k1, p1, k1, ssk, p1, k2tog, k1, (yo, k1) 3 times.

Row 3: k3, p5, k1, p2, k1, p2, k1, p5, k3, p1.

Row 4: sl1, k2tog, yo, k1, yo, k3, yo, ssk, p1, k2tog, p1, ssk, p1, k2tog, yo, k3, (yo, k1) 3 times.

Row 5: bind off 3, k2 (including st left on right needle after bind off), p8, k1, p8, k3, p1.

Row 6: sl1, k2tog, yo, k1, yo, k5, yo, sl1, k2tog, psso, p1, k3tog, yo, k5, (yo, k1) twice.

Row 7: k3, p8, k1, p8, k3, p1.

Row 8: sl1, k2tog, yo, k1, yo, k3, p1, k2tog, k1, yo, sl1, k2tog, psso, yo, k1, ssk, p1, k3, (yo, k1) 3 times.

Row 9: bind off 3, k2, p4, k1, p7, k1, p4, k3, p1.

☐	k on rs, p on ws	⃗	sl1, k2tog, psso
─	p on rs, k on ws	⃗	k3tog
O	yo	V	sl1 pwise with yarn at back
╱	k2tog	o	bind off 1
╲	ssk		

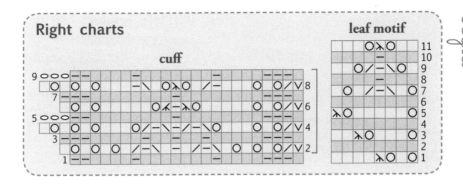

Right charts

leaf motif

Right mitt

With wrong side facing and working from right to left, pick up and knit 1 st in each slipped st along long straight edge of cuff. Pick up sts by inserting left needle tip from front to back under both strands of slipped st and k these strands tog as though they were a normal st. 29 [33] sts.

Without joining in the rnd turn.

Next row: (k1, kfb) to 1 st from end. Arrange sts evenly over 3 needles, or in 2 halves on a long circular for your preferred method of working small diameters in the rnd. K the last unworked picked up st tog with the 1st st. 42[48]sts. K10[12] rnds.

Next rnd: k16[18], pm, k to end.

Next rnd: k to marker,
yo, slm, k1, yo, k to end.

Next rnd: k to end.

Rep last 2 rnds 6[7] more times.

Next rnd: k16[18], slip next 15[17] sts onto scrap yarn (removing marker when you reach it), cable cast on 2 sts, k to end. 43[49] sts.

Next rnd: k6[8], work right leaf motif, k to end.

Rep last rnd 10 more times.

Next rnd: k.

Next rnd: k18[20], this will be the new beg of the rnd.

P1 rnd; k1 rnd; p1 rnd; bind off.

Right leaf motif

Rnd 1: yo, k1, yo, sl1, k2tog, psso, k4.

Rnds 2, 4, 6: k.

Rnd 3: yo, k3, yo, sl1, k2tog, psso, k2.

Rnd 5: yo, k5, yo, sl1, k2tog, psso.

Rnd 7: yo, k1, ssk, p1, k2tog, k1, yo, k1.

Rnds 8, 10: k3, p1, k4.

Rnd 9: k1, yo, ssk, p1, k2tog, yo, k2.

Rnd 11: k2, yo, sl1, k2tog, psso, yo, k3.

21

Right thumb

Return 15[17] held sts to needles; join yarn and pick up and k 4 sts from 2 cast on sts; divide these 19[21] sts evenly over needles; k around all held sts and 2 picked up sts; this will be the beg of the rnd.

Rnd 1: k1, k2tog, k to 3 sts from end, ssk, k1.

K4[6] rnds; p1 rnd; k1 rnd; p1 rnd; bind off.

Left cuff

Cast on 23 sts.

Row 1 (WS): k.

Row 2: (k3, yo, k2tog) 4 times, k2, p1.

Row 3: sl1, k to end.

Row 4: k to 1 st from end, p1.

Working from chart or written directions below work rows 1-8 of left cuff lace pattern 6[7]times, then work row 9 once.

Next row (RS): k to 1 st from end, p1.

Next row: sl1, k to end.

Rep last 2 rows once; bind off.

Left cuff lace pattern - written directions

Row 1 (WS): sl1, k3, p4, k1, p7, k1, p4, k1, yo, k1.

Row 2: k3, (yo, k1) twice, ssk, p1, k2tog, k1, p1, k1, ssk, p1, k2tog, (k1, yo) 3 times, ssk, p1.

Row 3: sl1, k3, p5, k1, p2, k1, p2, k1, p5, (k1, yo) twice, k1.

Row 4: bind off 3, k2, yo, k3, yo, ssk, p1, k2tog, p1, ssk, p1, k2tog, yo, k3, yo, k1, yo, ssk, p1.

Row 5: sl1, k3, p8, k1, p8, k1, yo, k1.

Row 6: k3, yo, k5, yo, sl1, k2tog, psso, p1, k3tog, yo, k5, yo, k1, yo, ssk, p1.

Row 7: sl1, k3, p8, k1, p8, (k1, yo) twice, k1.

Row 8: bind off 3, k2, yo, k3, p1, k2tog, k1, yo, sl1, k2tog, psso, yo, k1, ssk, p1, k3, yo, k1, yo, ssk, p1.

Row 9: sl1, k3, p4, k1, p7, k1, p4, k2.

☐ k on rs, p on ws		⅄ sl1, k2tog, psso
― p on rs, k on ws		⅄ k3tog
O yo		V sl1 pwise with yarn at back
╱ k2tog		⊙ bind off 1
╲ ssk		

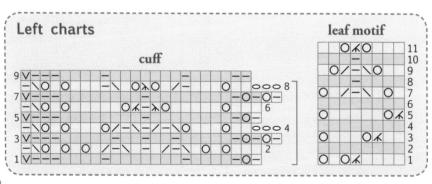

Left charts

cuff

leaf motif

Left mitt

With wrong side facing working from right to left, pick up and knit 1 st in each slipped st along long straight edge of cuff. Pick up sts by inserting left needle tip from front to back under both strands of slipped st and k these strands tog as though they were a normal st. 29[33] sts. Without joining in the rnd turn.

Next row: (k1, kfb) to 1 st from end. Arrange sts evenly over 3 needles, or in 2 halves on a long circular for your preferred method of working small diameters in the rnd. Position last unworked st at the beg of the 1st needle and work a ssk with this st and the 1st picked up st, the resulting st will be the 1st st in the rnd. 42[48] sts. K10[12] rnds.

Next rnd: k25[29], pm, k to end.

Next rnd: k to marker, yo, slm, k1, yo, k to end.

Next rnd: k to end.

Rep last 2 rnds 6[7] more times.

Next rnd: k25[29], slip next 15[17] sts onto scrap yarn (removing marker when you reach it), cable cast on 2 sts, k to end. 43[49] sts.

Next rnd: k29[31], work left leaf motif, k to end.

Rep last rnd 10 more times.

Next rnd: k.

Next rnd: k12[14], this will be the new beg of the rnd.

P1 rnd; k1 rnd; p1 rnd; bind off.

Left leaf motif

Rnd 1: k4, k3tog, yo, k1, yo.

Rnds 2, 4, 6: k.

Rnd 3: k2, k3tog, yo, k3, yo.

Rnd 5: k3tog, yo, k5, yo.

Rnd 7: k1, yo, k1, ssk, p1, k2tog, k1, yo.

Rnds 8, 10: k4, p1, k3.

Rnd 9: k2, yo, ssk, p1, k2tog, yo, k1.

Rnd 11: k3, yo, k3tog, yo, k2.

Left thumb work as for right thumb.

Finishing

Weave in ends, using end to close up any holes around picked up sts at thumb. Sew on buttons to match buttonholes, using either matching thread or a single ply of the yarn. Block, opening up the lace.

23

Snapdragon tam

A cosy tam featuring an allover lattice cable pattern, with petals (or perhaps they're little flames) that grow organically in the centre of each open section. Although the instructions look lengthy and the chart may seem a little daunting Snapdragon is surprisingly simple to knit, and of course you can work from either written or charted directions. Whether worked in a bright glowing colour or a cool neutral Snapdragon is a fun pattern that's sure to cheer up dreary winter days and would make a perfect gift.

Notes

Refer to table on following page for stitch counts. Stitch counts are given for every round that changes the number of stitches and show the total stitch count at the end of the rnd.

Materials

180[220, 260]yds / 165[200, 240]m light worsted (dk) weight yarn.
Shown in Madelinetosh Tosh DK (100% superwash merino, 225yds / 206m, 3.52 /100g) in Gilded.
Size 6 US / 4mm 16" / 40cm circular
Size 6 US / 4mm dpns
Marker, a removable marker will make things easier.

Gauge

20 sts and 28 rnds = 4" / 10cm in st st

Sizes

s[m, l] - to fit size - 18[22, 26]" / 46[56, 66]cm,
finished circumference 16[20, 24]" / 41[51, 61]cm
Shown in size M (2" of negative ease). For a looser, slouchier hat, work a larger size which may make band too loose. This can be counteracted by working it on smaller needles or threading elastic through at the end.

Rnd	s	m	l
1	88	110	132
10	120	150	180
18	112	140	168
19	120	150	180
24	152	190	228
30	136	170	204
32	128	160	192
33	120	150	180
38	152	190	228
44	136	170	204
45	132	166	200
46	112	140	168
47	108	135	162
48	100	125	150
49	92	115	138
50	84	105	126
52	100	125	150
58	92	115	138
59	84	105	126
60	80	100	120
61	72	90	108
62	64	80	96
63	56	70	84
64	48	60	72
68	32	40	48
69	24	30	36
70	16	20	24
71	8	10	12

Directions

With circular cast on 88[110, 132] sts, join rnd, placing marker to mark the beg of the rnd. Work rnds 1-71 from either chart or written directions below, switching to dpns when there are too few sts to comfortably fit on circular.

Written directions

Rnds 1-7: *(p2, k2) twice, p2, k1; rep from * to end.

Rnd 8: *p2, T3F, T3B, p2, k1; rep from * to end.

Rnd 9: *p3, k4, p3, k1; rep from * to end.

Rnd 10: *p3, C4B, p3, inc 4; rep from * to end.

Rnds 11-15: *p3, k4, p3, k5; rep from * to end.

Rnd 16: *p3, C4B, p3, T2F, k1, T2B; rep from * to end.

Rnd 17: p3, k2, move marker to this point to mark the new beg of the rnd, *k2, p4, k3, p4, k2; rep from * to end.

Rnd 18: *T3F, p3, sl1, k2, psso, p3, T3B; rep from * to end.

Rnd 19: *p1, k2, p8, k2, p1, m1; rep from * to end.

Rnd 20: *p1, T4F, p4, T4B, p1, k1; rep from * to end.

Rnd 21: *p3, k2, p4, k2, p3, k1; rep from * to end.

Rnd 22: *p3, T4F, T4B, p3, k1; rep from * to end.

Rnd 23: *p5, k4, p5, k1; rep from * to end.

Rnd 24: *p5, C4F, p5, inc 4; rep from * to end.

Rnds 25-29: *p5, k4, p5, k5; rep from * to end.

Rnd 30: *p5, C4F, p5, ssk, k1, k2tog; rep from * to end.

Rnd 31: *p5, k4, p5, k3; rep from * to 10 sts from end, move marker to this point to mark the new beg of the rnd.

Rnd 32: *T3F, p4, sl1, k2, psso, p4, T3B; rep from * to end.

Rnd 33: *p1, k1, ssk, p8, k2tog, k1, p1, m1; rep from * to end.

Rnd 34: *p1, T4F, p4, T4B, p1, k1; rep from * to end.

Rnd 35: *p3, k2, p4, k2, p3, k1; rep from * to end.

Rnd 36: *p3, T4F, T4B, p3, k1; rep from * to end.

Rnd 37: *p5, k4, p5, k1; rep from * to end.

Rnd 38: *p5, C4B, p5, inc 4; rep from * to end.

Rnds 39-43: *p5, k4, p5, k5; rep from * to end.

Rnd 44: *p5, C4B, p5, ssk, k1, k2tog; rep from * to end.

Rnd 45: p5, k2, move marker to this point to mark the new beg of the rnd, *k1, ssk, p4, k3, p4, k2tog, k1; rep from * to end.

Rnd 46: *T3F, p3, sl1, k2, psso, p3, T3B; rep from * to end.

Rnd 47: *p1, k1, ssk, p7, k2, p1, m1, p1, k2, p7, k2tog, k1, p1; rep from * to end.

Rnd 48: *p1, k1, ssk, p4, T4B, p1, k1, p1, T4F, p4, k2tog, k1, p1; rep from * to end.

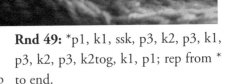

Rnd 49: *p1, k1, ssk, p3, k2, p3, k1, p3, k2, p3, k2tog, k1, p1; rep from * to end.

Rnd 50: *p1, k1, ssk, T4B, p3, k1, p3, T4F, k2tog, k1, p1; rep from * to end.

Rnd 51: *p1, k4, p5, k1, p5, k4, p1; rep from * to end.

Rnd 52: *p1, C4F, p5, inc 4, p5, C4F, p1; rep from * to end.

Rnds 53-57: *p1, k4, p5, k5, p5, k4, p1; rep from * to end.

Rnd 58: *p1, C4F, p5, ssk, k1, k2tog, p5, C4F, p1; rep from * to end.

Rnd 59: *p1, k3, ssk, p4, k3, p4, k2tog, k3, p1; rep from * to 3 sts from end, move marker to this point to mark the new beg of the rnd.

Rnd 60: *k2, p2, k2, T3F, p3, sl1, k2, psso, p3, T3B; rep from * to end.

Rnd 61: *k2, p2, k2, p1, k1, ssk, p6, k2tog, k1, p1; rep from * to end.

Rnd 62: *T3F, T3B, p1, k1, ssk, p4, k2tog, k1, p1; rep from * to end.

Rnd 63: *p1, k4, p2, k1, ssk, p2, k2tog, k1, p1; rep from * to end.

Rnd 64: *p1, k4, p2, k1, ssk, k2tog, k1, p1; rep from * to end.

Rnd 65: *p1, k4, p1; rep from * to end.

Rnd 66: *p1, C4B, p1; rep from * to end.

Rnd 67: *p1, k4, p1; rep from * to end.

Rnd 68: *k2tog, k2, ssk; rep from * to end.

Rnd 69: *k1, k2tog, k1; rep from * to end.

Rnd 70: *k2tog, k1; rep from * to end.

Rnd 71: k2tog to end.

Finishing

Break yarn and draw through rem 8[10, 12] sts, pulling up tightly and fastening securely on the inside. Weave in ends and block over an appropriately sized disk, such as a dinner plate. Since the stitch count changes so frequently blocking well is crucial to opening up the pattern and achieving the right shape.

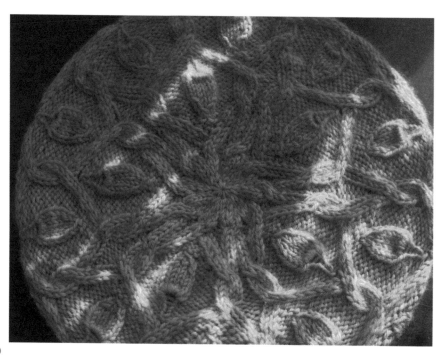

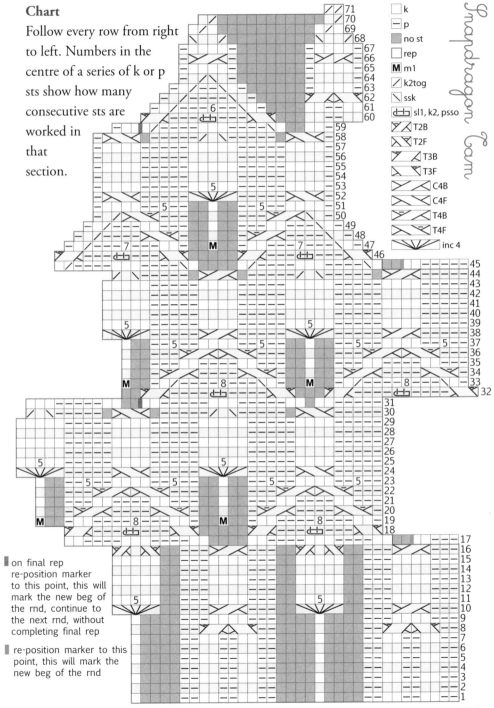

Chart

Follow every row from right to left. Numbers in the centre of a series of k or p sts show how many consecutive sts are worked in that section.

Legend:
- □ k
- − p
- ▓ no st
- □ rep
- M m1
- ╱ k2tog
- ╲ ssk
- ⊞ sl1, k2, psso
- T2B
- T2F
- T3B
- T3F
- C4B
- C4F
- T4B
- T4F
- inc 4

▌ on final rep re-position marker to this point, this will mark the new beg of the rnd, continue to the next rnd, without completing final rep

▌ re-position marker to this point, this will mark the new beg of the rnd

Grandragon Yarn

29

Snapdragon flip-tops

Fun and highly practical mittens with flip-tops that will keep your fingers toasty warm but allow them to make a quick escape when you need to unlock the door or button your coat. The cable and petal pattern on the cuffs grows into an elegant motif on the back of the hand that invisibly incorporates the necessary shaping for the thumb. Picking up stitches for the flip-tops has the potential to look messy but detailed instructions are provided for a method that looks virtually seamless.

Materials

180yds / 165m light worsted (dk) weight yarn.
Shown in Madelinetosh Tosh DK (100% superwash merino, 225yds / 206m, 3.52 /100g) in Gilded.
Size 6 US / 4mm dpns
Scrap yarn for holding sts

Gauge

20 sts and 28 rnds = 4" / 10cm in st st

Sizes

The mittens are very stretchy, particularly at the cuffs and should easily fit hands measuring 7-8.5" / 18-22cm around knuckles. The length can be simply adjusted to fit and where to do this is indicated in the pattern.

Directions

Cuff - both mitts

Cast on 44 sts.
Working from either written directions or chart work 40 rnds of cuff pattern.

Hand

R mitt: k 1 rnd; k19, slip next 10 sts onto scrap yarn, cable cast on 2 sts, k to end.

L mitt: k to 8 sts from end of rnd, slip next 10 sts onto scrap yarn, this will be the new beg of the rnd, cable cast on 2 sts onto needle 1, k to end.

Both mitts: k 7 rnds.
Work 8 rnds of p2, k2 ribbing.
Bind off in pattern; break yarn.

Flip top

Using darning needle thread tail of yarn from outside of the mitt to the inside. Pick up and knit the 22 sts shown in illustration by inserting a dpn into each stitch all the way through the fabric and catch the tail of yarn on the inside of the mitt. Pull a loop through to the right side, making sure to leave a long enough tail before the 1st st to allow for weaving in. Pull any extra yarn back through to right side and cable cast on 16 sts, divide these sts evenly between 2 dpns; join rnd. 38 sts.

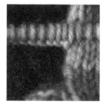

1. bring long tail of working yarn to inside between these 2 sts

2. insert dpn into the centre of this st, catch yarn on inside and pull loop through

3. pick up rem 21 shaded sts in the same way as the first, working from right to left

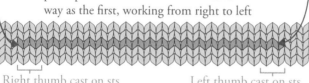

Right thumb cast on sts   Left thumb cast on sts

Next 6 rnds: k 23, (p2, k2) to 3 sts from end, p2, k1.

K 19 rnds or until mitten top is 1.5" / 4cm shorter than desired length.

K 2 sts from needle 1 onto needle 3 and slip last 2 sts on needle 1 onto needle 2.

18 sts on needle 1 and 10 sts each on needles 2 and 3.

Next rnd: ssk, k to 2 sts from end of needle 1, k2tog, k1, ssk, k to 3 sts from end of rnd, k2tog, k1.

Next rnd: k.

Rep last 2 rnds until 10 sts rem.

Next rnd: ssk, k2tog, k1, ssk, k2tog, k1.

Slip rem 6 sts onto 1 needle so that the 1st st of the rnd is closest to the right tip; k2tog 3 times. Work I-cord on these 3 sts: *k3, slide sts to other end of dpn without turning, rep from * for 14 rows; bind off.

Thumb

Return 10 held sts to needles; join yarn and pick up and k 4 sts from 2 cast on sts; divide these 14 sts evenly over needles.

K 16 rnds or until thumb is 0.5" / 1cm shorter than desired length.

Next rnd: (k2, k2tog) 3 times, k2.

Next rnd: (k1, k2tog) 3 times, k2.

Next rnd: k2tog around. Break yarn and draw through rem 4 sts, pulling up tightly and fastening securely on the inside.

Finishing
Sew bound off edge of I-cord to base to make button loop; weave in ends; sew button to cuff. Block.

Cuff pattern - written directions
Rnds 1-7: *(p2, k2) twice, p2, k1; rep from * to end.

Rnd 8: *p2, T3F, T3B, p2, k1; rep from * to end.

Rnd 9: *p3, k4, p3, k1; rep from * to end.

Rnd 10: *p3, C4B, p3, inc 4; rep from * to end.

Rnds 11-15: *p3, k4, p3, k5; rep from * to end.

Rnd 16: *p3, C4B, p3, T2F, k1, T2B; rep from * to end.

Rnd 17: p3, k2, slip the 5 sts just worked onto needle 3, this will now be the beg of the rnd, *k2, p4, k3, p4, k2; rep from * to end.

Rnd 18: *T3F, p3, sl1, k2, psso, p3, T3B; rep from * to end.

Rnd 19: p1, k2, p8, k2, p1, m1, *p1, k2, p8, k2, p1; rep from * to end.

Rnd 20: p1, T4F, p4, T4B, p1, k1, * p1, T4F, p4, T4B, p1; rep from * to end.

Rnd 21: p3, k1, ssk, p2, k2tog, k1, p3, k1, *p3, k1, ssk, p2, k2tog, k1, p3, m1; rep from * to end.

Rnd 22: m1, p3, k1, ssk, k2tog, k1, p3, k1, p3, k1, ssk, k2tog, k1, p3, m1, k1, *m1, p3, k1, ssk, k2tog, k1, p3, m1, k1; rep from * to end.

Rnd 23: m1, k1, p3, k1, k2tog, k1, p3, k1, p3, k1, ssk, k1, p3, k1, m1, k1, *m1, k1, p3, k1, k2tog, k1, p3, k1, m1, k1; rep from * to end.

Rnd 24: k1, m1, k1, p3, k2tog, k1, p3, inc4, p3, k1, ssk, p3, k1, m1, k2, *k1, m1, k1, p3, sl1, k2tog, psso, p3, k1, m1, k2; rep from * to end.

Rnd 25: k3, p3, k2, p3, k5, p3, k2, p3, k4, *k2, C2F, p5, C2B, k3; rep from * to end.

Rnd 26: k3, p3, k2, p3, k5, p3, k2, p3, k4, *k3, C2F, p3, C2B, k4; rep from * to end.

Rnd 27: k3, p3, k2, p3, k5, p3, k2, p3, k4, *k4, C2F, k1, C2B, k5; rep from * to end.

Rnd 28: k3, p3, k2, p3, k5, p3, k2, p3, k4*k6, k2tog, k6; rep from * to end.

Rnd 29: k3, p3, k2, p3, k5, p3, k2, p3, k to end.

Rnd 30: k3, p3, k2, p3, T2F, k1, T2B, p3, k2, p3, k to end.

Rnd 31: k3, p3, k2, p4, k3, p4, k2, p3, k to end.

Rnd 32: k2, C2F, p2, T3F, p3, sl1, k2, psso, p3, T3B, p2, C2B, k to end.

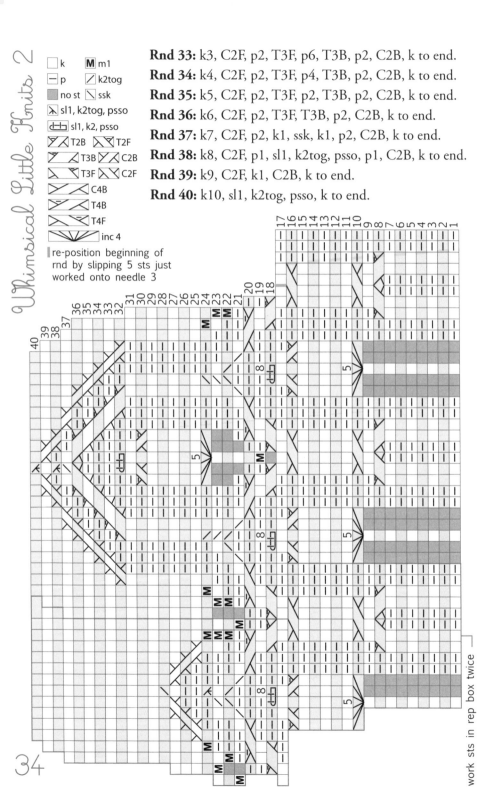

Whimsical Little Knits 2

Key:
- □ k
- M m1
- − p
- ╱ k2tog
- ▨ no st
- ╲ ssk
- ⅄ sl1, k2tog, psso
- ⎓ sl1, k2, psso
- T2B / T2F
- T3B / C2B
- T3F / C2F
- C4B
- T4B
- T4F
- inc 4

| re-position beginning of rnd by slipping 5 sts just worked onto needle 3

Rnd 33: k3, C2F, p2, T3F, p6, T3B, p2, C2B, k to end.
Rnd 34: k4, C2F, p2, T3F, p4, T3B, p2, C2B, k to end.
Rnd 35: k5, C2F, p2, T3F, p2, T3B, p2, C2B, k to end.
Rnd 36: k6, C2F, p2, T3F, T3B, p2, C2B, k to end.
Rnd 37: k7, C2F, p2, k1, ssk, k1, p2, C2B, k to end.
Rnd 38: k8, C2F, p1, sl1, k2tog, psso, p1, C2B, k to end.
Rnd 39: k9, C2F, k1, C2B, k to end.
Rnd 40: k10, sl1, k2tog, psso, k to end.

work sts in rep box twice

34

Emily

Ever since I first encountered Emily Martin's (http://theblackapple.typepad.com/) work I've dreamed of knitting an adorable, Emily inspired, capelet. Worked from side to side and shaped with simple short row wedges the capelet features a neat integrated I-cord edging around the neck and a deep lace and cable pattern around the gently flared bottom edge. The yarn used is perfect in garter stitch, so light and lofty that you'll forget you're wearing it, but whether at the ball or the supermarket it will keep your shoulders warm and add a little fairytale romance to your outfit.

Materials

33yds / 30m **per repeat** of heavy fingering to light worsted weight yarn (the yarn used is very lofty and fills in the spaces when knit loosely, use a yarn that gives you a fabric you like at the correct gauge). Shown in Imperial Stock Ranch Sock (100% wool, 545 yds / 498 m, 4oz / 113g) in natural. Size 7 US / 4.5 mm needles, 3 small buttons.

Gauge 17sts and 36rows = 4" / 10cm in garter st

Sizes

The simplest way to size the capelet is to knit until you're happy with the fit, but in case your intended wearer isn't handy for constant try ons a table of the number of repeats to work for bust sizes between 30 - 56" / 76 - 142cm is given. Length is 13" /33cm but can easily be altered by changing the number of sts cast on and working according to the pattern. Up to 8 sts can be removed before there will be problems with the shaping.

Directions

Cast on 52 sts. Working from either written or charted instructions work rows 1-26, then repeat rows 3-26 until the total number of repeats shown have been worked or the desired fit has been acheived. Work rows 3-6 once more. Bind off all sts.

Size	30" 76cm	32 81.5 cm	34 86.5 cm	36 91.5 cm	38 96.5 cm	40 101.5 cm	42 106.5 cm
Reps	13	14	15	16	17	18	19

Size	44 112cm	46 117cm	48 122cm	50 127cm	52 132cm	54 137cm	56 142cm
Reps	20	21	22	23	24	25	26

Written directions

Row 1 (WS): k6, p4, k1, pm, k to 3 sts from end, p3.

Row 2: sl3, (yo, k2tog, k2) 3 times, k to marker, slm, p1, k5, (yo, ssk) twice, yo, k1.

Row 3: k3, (yo, ssk) twice, p4, k1, slm, k to 3 sts from end, p3.

Row 4: sl3, k to marker, slm, p1, C4B, k1, (yo, ssk) twice, (yo, k1) twice.

Row 5: k5, (yo, ssk) twice, p4, k1, slm, k to 3 sts from end, p3.

Row 6: sl3, k to marker, slm, p1, k5, (yo, ssk) twice, k to end.

Row 7: bo3, k2, (yo, ssk) twice, p4, k1, slm, k to 3 sts from end, p3.

Row 8: sl3, k to marker, slm, p1, k2, yo, k3, (yo, ssk) twice, yo, k1.

Row 9: k3, (yo, ssk) twice, p5, k1, slm, k to 5 sts from end, w+t.

Row 10: k to marker, slm, p1, k2, yo, k1, yo, k3, (yo, ssk) twice, (yo, k1) twice.

Row 11: k5, (yo, ssk) twice, p7, k1, slm, k to 4 sts before wrapped st, w+t.

Row 12: k to marker, slm, p1, k2, (yo, k3) twice, (yo, ssk) twice, k to end.

Row 13: bo3, k2, (yo, ssk) twice, p9, k1, slm, k to 4 sts before wrapped st, w+t.

Row 14: k to marker, slm, p1, k2, yo, k2, yo, ssk, k1, yo, k3, (yo, ssk) twice, yo, k1.

Row 15: k3, (yo, ssk) twice, p11, k1, slm, k to 4 sts before wrapped st, w+t.

Row 16: k to marker, slm, p1, k2, yo, k1, k2tog, yo, k1, yo, ssk, k1, yo, k3, (yo, ssk) twice, (yo, k1) twice.

Row 17: k5, (yo, ssk) twice, p13, k1, slm, k to 4 sts before wrapped st, w+t.

Row 18: k to marker, slm, p1, k1, ssk, yo, ssk, k1, yo, k2tog twice, yo, k2tog, k2, (yo, ssk) twice, k to end.

Row 19: bo3, k2, (yo, ssk) twice, p11, k1, slm, k to 4 sts before wrapped st, w+t.

Row 20: k to marker, slm, p1, k1, ssk, yo, ssk, k1, k2tog, yo, k2tog, k2, (yo, ssk) twice, yo, k1.

Row 21: k3, (yo, ssk) twice, p9, k1, slm, k to 4 sts before wrapped st, w+t.

Row 22: k to marker, slm, p1, k1, ssk, yo, sl1, k2tog, psso, yo, k2tog, k2, (yo, ssk) twice, (yo, k1) twice.

Row 23: k5, (yo, ssk) twice, p7, k1, slm, k to 4 sts before wrapped st, w+t.

Row 24: k to marker, slm, p1, k1, ssk, yo, k3tog, k2, (yo, ssk) twice, k to end.

Row 25: bo3, k2, (yo, ssk) twice, p5, k1, slm, k to 3 sts from end working wrapped sts without picking up wraps, p3.

Row 26: sl3, k to marker, slm, p1, k2, k2tog, k2, (yo, ssk) twice, yo, k1.

Finishing

Weave in ends. Block, opening up lace and shaping bottom edge into gentle scallops. Sew on buttons to correspond with buttonholes.

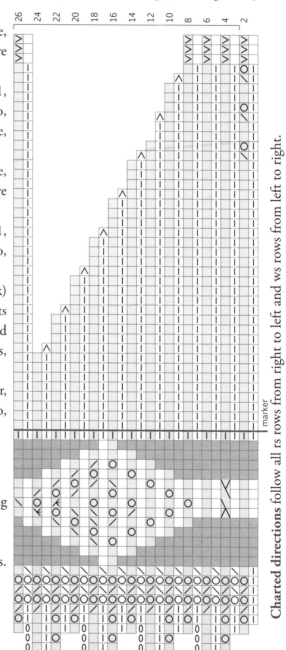

Charted directions follow all rs rows from right to left and ws rows from left to right.

Nathaniel

Adorable squirrel shaped cushion that will bring a little woodland whimsy to your home. He's fun to knit, although he's made of 2 flat silhouettes with a garter stitch strip between them he's knit seamlessly in the rnd. Nathaniel is just the right size to be a cozy, functional cushion that also looks wonderful propped on a bed or chair when you're not squashing him.

Materials

220yds / 200m bulky weight yarn.
Shown in O-wool Legacy Bulky (100% organic wool, 106 yds / 97m, 3.53oz /100g) in Russet.
Size 10 US / 6 mm 24"/ 60cm circ and dpns.
Stuffing, I stuffed him with wool fibre which is pleasingly heavy and warms with your body, but you could use any toy stuffing.

Gauge 12 sts and 20 rnds = 4" / 10cm in st st

Size approx 18" tall and 12" across.

Directions

Base

Provisionally cast on 8 sts.
Row 1: sl1, k6, p1.
Rep row 1 59 more times, 30 slipped sts on each side.

Without turning at the end of final row pick up and k 30 sts down closest vertical edge. Undo provisional cast on and slip resulting 8 sts onto left needle tip, k across them, then pick up and k 30 sts along 2nd vertical edge. Turn.

K 31, pm, p6, pm, k32, pm, p6, place unique marker, this will now be the beginning of the rnd.

Work 59 rnds of body from either written directions or chart. If working from chart, work every rnd as follows: follow chart from right to left to marker, slm, work 6 sts in garter st, slm, follow chart from left to right to marker, slm, work 6 sts in garter st. When following the chart from left to right mirror increases and decreases.

Separating head and tail
K to marker, slm, p6, slm, k22, slip the next 36 sts onto scrap yarn, pm, cable cast on 6, pm. Divide the resulting 56 live sts evenly onto dpns and join rnd. Work head from written directions or chart.

Completing ear
After working head complete ear as follows:
Next rnd - remove markers as you come to them: sl1, k2tog, psso, k6, k3tog, k6.
Next rnd: p2tog, p5, p2tog, p5.

Stuff body and head.
Arrange 6 sts from each side on 2 dpns and use a 3rd dpn to work a 3 needle bind off.

Tail
Return held sts to dpns. With head to the left join yarn pm and pick up and k 6 sts from cast on sts for head, pm, k to marker, p6. Work tail from either written directions or chart.

Completing tail
After working head complete tail as follows:
Next rnd - remove markers as you come to them: ssk, k2tog, k6, ssk, k2tog, k5, p2tog twice, p4, p2tog twice, p4.
Stuff tail.
Arrange 6 sts from each side on 2 dpns and use a 3rd dpn to work a 3 needle bind off.

Finishing - bury ends securely on inside.

Written Directions
Body
Rnd 1: k.
Rnd 2: (k to marker, slm, p6, slm) twice.
Rnd 3: k.
Rnd 4: k2, LLI, k to 3 sts before marker, k2tog, k1, slm, p6, slm, k1, ssk, k to 2 sts from marker, RLI, k2, slm, p6.

Rnds 5-6: k to 3 sts before marker, k2tog, k1, slm, g6, slm, k1, ssk, k to marker, slm, g6.

Rnd 7: work even in patt.

Rnd 8: k2, LLI, k to marker, slm, p6, slm, k to 2 sts from marker, RLI, k2, slm, p6.

Rnd 9: work even in patt.

Rnd 10: k to 2 sts from marker, RLI, k2, slm, p6, slm, k2, LLI, k to marker, slm, p6.

Rnd 11: work even in patt.

Rnd 12: (k2, LLI, k to 2 sts from marker, RLI, k2, slm, p6, slm) twice.

Rnd 13: work even in patt.

Rnd 14: k to 2 sts from marker, RLI, k2, slm, p6, slm, k2, LLI, k to marker, slm, p6.

Rnds 15-21: work even in patt.

Rnds 22-25: k to 3 sts before marker, k2tog, k1, slm, g6, slm, k1, ssk, k to marker, slm, g6.

Rnds 26-31: work even in patt.

Rnd 32: k1, ssk, k to marker, slm, p6, slm, k to 3 sts before marker, k2tog, k1, slm, p6.

Rnd 33: work even in patt.

Rnds 34-35: k to 2 sts from marker, RLI, k2, slm, g6, slm, k2, LLI, k to marker, slm, g6.

Rnd 36: k1, ssk, k to 2 sts from marker, RLI, k2, slm, p6, slm, k2, LLI, k to 3 sts from marker, k2tog, k1, slm, p6.

Rnds 37-38: k to 2 sts from marker, RLI, k2, slm, g6, slm, k2, LLI, k to marker, slm, g6.

Rnd 39: work even in patt.

Rnd 40: k1, ssk, k to 2 sts from marker, RLI, k2, slm, p6, slm, k2, LLI, k to 3 sts from marker, k2tog, k1, slm, p6.

Rnd 41: work even in patt.

Rnd 42: k to 2 sts from marker, RLI, k2, slm, p6, slm, k2, LLI, k to marker, slm, p6.

Rnd 43: work even in patt.

Rnd 44: k1, ssk, k to marker, slm, p6, slm, k to 3 sts before marker, k2tog, k1, slm, p6.

Rnd 45: work even in patt.

Rnds 46-47: k to 3 sts before marker, k2tog, k1, slm, g6, slm, k1, ssk, k to marker, slm, g6.

Rnd 48: k1, ssk, k to 3 sts before marker, k2tog, k1, slm, p6, slm, k1, ssk, k to 3 sts before marker, k2tog, k1, slm, p6.

Rnds 49-50: k to 3 sts before marker, k2tog, k1, slm, g6, slm, k1, ssk, k to marker, slm, g6.

Rnd 51: work even in patt.

Rnds 52-57: k to 2 sts from marker, RLI, k2, slm, g6, slm, k2, LLI, k to marker, slm, g6.

Rnd 58: k2, LLI, k to 2 sts from marker, RLI, k2, slm, p6, slm, k2, LLI, k to 2 sts from marker, RLI, k2, slm, p6.

Rnd 59: k to 2 sts from marker, RLI, k2, slm, k6, slm, k2, LLI, k to marker, slm, k6.

Head

Rnd 1: k.

Rnd 2: k1, ssk, k to marker, slm, p6, slm, k to 3 sts before marker, k2tog, k1, slm, p6.

Rnd 3: work even in patt.

Rnds 4-9: rep rnds 2-3 3 more times.

Rnd 10: (k1, ssk, k to 3 sts before marker, k2tog, k1, slm, p6, slm) twice.

Rnds 11: work even in patt.

Rnds 12-13: rep rnds 10-11.

Rnd 14: (k1, ssk, k to 3 sts before marker, k2tog, k1, slm, p6, slm) twice.

Rnds 15-18: k to 3 sts before marker, k2tog, k1, slm, g6, slm, k1, ssk, k to marker, slm, g6.

Rnds 19-20: k to 4 sts before marker, k3tog, k1, slm, g6, slm, k1, sl1, k2tog, psso, k to marker, slm, g6.

Rnd 21: work even in patt.

Rnd 22: k1, ssk, k1, slm, p6, slm, k1, k2tog, k1, slm, p6.

Tail

Rnd 1: k.

Rnd 2: k2, LLI, k to marker, slm, p6, slm, k to 2 sts from marker, RLI, k2, slm, p6.

Rnds 3-5: work even in patt.

Rnds 6-13: rep rns 2-5 twice more.

Rnd 14: k2, LLI, k to 3 sts before marker, k2tog, k1, slm, p6, slm, k1, ssk, k to 2 sts from marker, RLI, k2, slm, p6.

Rnd 15: work even in patt.

Rnd 16: k2, LLI, k to marker, slm, p6, slm, k to 2 sts from marker, RLI, k2, slm, p6.

Rnd 17: work even in patt.

Rnd 18: k2, LLI, k to 3 sts before marker, k2tog, k1, slm, p6, slm, k1, ssk, k to 2 sts from marker, RLI, k2, slm, p6.

Rnds 19-21: work even in patt.

Rnd 22: k to 3 sts before marker, k2tog, k1, slm, p6, slm, k1, ssk, k to marker, slm, p6.

Rnd 23: work even in patt.

Rnds 24-25: rep rnds 22-23.

Rnd 26: k1, ssk, k to 3 sts before marker, k2tog, k1, slm, p6, slm, k1, ssk, k to 3 sts before marker, k2tog, k1, slm, p6.

Rnd 27: k to 3 sts before marker, k2tog, k1, slm, k6, slm, k1, ssk, k to marker, slm, k6.

Rnd 28: (k1, ssk, k to 3 sts before marker, k2tog, k1, slm, p6, slm) twice.

Rnd 29: (k1, sl1, k2tog, psso, k4, k3tog, k1, slm, k6, slm) twice.

Rnd 30: (k1, sl1, k2tog, psso, k3tog, k1, slm, k6, slm) twice.

Nathaniel chart

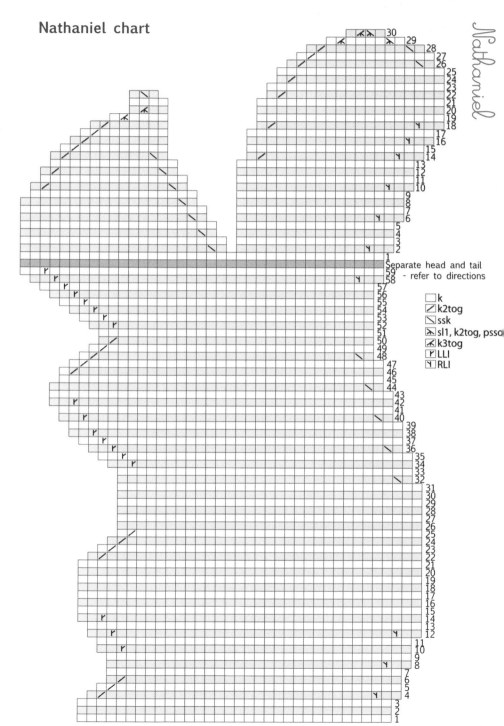

Separate head and tail
- refer to directions

□ k
⊿ k2tog
◹ ssk
⬟ sl1, k2tog, psso
⬩ k3tog
⊮ LLI
⊻ RLI

43

Peaks Island Hood

A hooded scarf that's designed to look equally good with the hood up or down. The ends feature a simple shell pattern that's echoed in the hood shaping and that can be worked in either direction which means that the whole thing is worked in one piece. One end of the scarf is longer than the other to be wrapped around your neck once and the crossed over ends are fastened with a few pretty vintage buttons, keeping the chills away from your chest without any extra bulk.

Notes

When directed to work in patt work the sts as they appear on the needle, k the ks and p the ps, except when working in seed st, when sts presenting as k should be purled and vice versa.

Work 1 row buttonhole over 3 sts as follows: bring yarn to front, sl1 pwise, bring yarn to back, (sl1 pwise, psso) twice, sl last st back to left needle, turn work and cable cast on 2 sts onto left needle, cast on 1 more st but bring yarn to front before placing stitch on left needle, turn work again, sl1 kwise, pass last cast on st over sl st, k1.

Directions

Left side of scarf

Cast on 45 sts.

Row 1 (WS): p2, (k4, p1) twice, p1, (k4, p1) 4 times, p1, (k4, p1) twice, p1.

Row 2: sl1, k1, (p4, k1) twice, pm, m1, pm, k1, (p4, k1) 4 times, pm, m1, pm, k1, (p4, k1) twice, p1. 47 sts.

Row 3: sl1, p1, (k4, p1) twice, slm, k1, slm, p1, (k4, p1) 4 times, slm, k1, slm, p1, (k4, p1) twice, p1.

Materials

470yds / 430m worsted weight yarn.

Shown in Green Mountain Spinnery Mountain Mohair (70% wool, 30% mohair, 140 yds / 128 m, 2oz /57g) in Ice Blue.

Size 10 US / 6mm needles.

3 buttons approx 1" / 2.5cm in diameter.

Gauge

16 sts and 20 rows = 4" / 10cm in seed st

Row 4: (work in patt to marker, slm, m1, p1, m1, slm) twice, work in patt to end. 51 sts.

Row 5: sl1, p1, (k1, k2tog, k1, p1) twice, slm, k1, p1, k1, slm, p1, (k1, k2tog, k1, p1) 4 times, slm, k1, p1, k1, slm, p1, (k1, k2tog, k1, p1) twice, p1. 43 sts.

Row 6: (work in patt to marker, slm, m1, ss to marker, m1, slm) twice, work in patt to end. 47 sts.

Row 7: work in patt to end.

Row 8: rep row 6. 51 sts.

Row 9: sl1, p1, (k1, k2tog, p1) twice, slm, ss to marker, slm, p1, (k1, k2tog, p1) 4 times, slm, ss to marker, slm, p1, (k1, k2tog, p1) twice, p1. 43 sts.

Row 10: rep row 6. 47 sts.

Row 11: work in patt to end.

Row 12: rep row 6. 51 sts.

Row 13: sl1, p1, (k2tog, p1) twice, slm, ss to marker, slm, p1, (k2tog, p1) 4 times, slm, ss to marker, slm, p1, (k2tog, p1) twice, p1. 43 sts.

Row 14: rep row 6. 47 sts.

Row 15: work in patt to end.

Row 16: sl1, k1, k2tog twice, slm, ss to marker, slm, ssk twice, k1, k2tog twice, slm, ss to marker, slm, ssk twice, k1, p1. 39 sts.

Row 17: work in patt to end.

Row 18: sl1, k1, k2tog, slm, ss to marker, slm, ssk, k1, k2tog, slm, ss to marker, slm, ssk, k1, p1. 35 sts.

Row 19: work in patt to end.

Row 20: sl1, k2tog, slm, ss to marker, slm, sl1, k2tog, psso, slm, ss to marker, slm, ssk, p1. 31 sts.

Row 21: sl1, ss to end removing markers as you come to them.

Continuing to sl the 1st st and p the last st of every row work in patt for 28" / 71cm more ending with a RS row.

Hood increases

Row 1 (WS): work 7 sts in patt, pm, work in patt to end.

Row 2 (RS): work in patt to marker, slm, m1, k1, m1, pm, work in patt to end. 33 sts.

Row 3: work in patt to marker, slm, p to marker, slm, work in patt to end.

Row 4: work in patt to marker, slm, (k1, m1) twice, k1, slm, work in patt to end. 35 sts.

Row 5: work in patt to marker, slm, p to marker, slm, work in patt to end.

Row 6: work in patt to marker, slm, (k1, m1p) 4 times, k1, slm, work in patt to end. 39 sts.

Work 3 rows in patt.

Row 10: work in patt to marker, slm, (k1, p1, m1p) 4 times, k1, slm, work in patt to end. 43 sts.

Work 3 rows in patt.

Row 14: work in patt to marker, slm, (k1, p1, m1p, p1) 4 times, k1, slm, work in patt to end. 47 sts.

Work 3 rows in patt.

Row 18: work in patt to marker, slm, (k1, p1, m1p, p2) 4 times, k1, slm, work in patt to end. 51 sts.
Work 3 rows in patt.
Row 22: work in patt to marker, slm, (k1, p1, m1p, p3) 4 times, k1, slm, work in patt to end. 55 sts.
Work 3 rows in patt.
Row 26: work in patt to marker, slm, (k1, p1, m1p, p4) 4 times, k1, slm, work in patt to end. 59 sts.
Work 3 rows in patt.
Row 30: work in patt to marker, slm, work 7 sts in seed st, work in patt to 7 sts before marker, work in seed st to marker beg with a p st, slm, work in patt to end.
Work 3 rows in patt.
Row 34: work in patt to marker, slm, work 14 sts in seed st, k1, work in seed st to marker beg with a k st, slm, work in patt to end. Work 3 rows in patt.
Row 38: work in ss to end.
Continuing to sl the 1st st and p the last st of every row work in patt for 9" / 23cm ending with a WS row.

Hood decreases

Row 1 (RS): work in patt to marker, slm, work 14 sts in patt, k1, work in patt to end. Work 3 rows in patt.

Row 5: work in patt to marker, slm, work 7 sts in patt, (k1, p6) twice, k1, work in patt to end.
Work 3 rows in patt.

Row 9: work in patt to marker, slm, (k1, p6) 4 times, k1, work in patt to end. Work 4 rows in patt.

Row 14 (WS): work in patt to marker, slm, (p1, k3, k2tog, k1) 4 times, p1, work in patt to end. 55 sts.
Work 3 rows in patt.

Row 18: work in patt to marker, slm, (p1, k2, k2tog, k1) 4 times, p1, work in patt to end. 51 sts.

Work 3 rows in patt.

Row 22: work in patt to marker, slm, (p1, k1, k2tog, k1) 4 times, p1, work in patt to end. 47 sts.
Work 3 rows in patt.

Row 26: work in patt to marker, slm, (p1, k1, k2tog) 4 times, p1, work in patt to end. 43 sts.
Work 3 rows in patt.

Row 30: work in patt to marker, slm, (p1, k2tog) 4 times, p1, work in patt to end. 39 sts.
Work 2 rows in patt.

Row 33 (RS): work in patt to marker, slm, ssk twice, k1, k2tog twice, work in patt to end. 35 sts. Work 1 row in patt.

Row 35: work in patt to marker, slm, ssk, k1, k2tog, work in patt to end. Work 1 row in patt. 33 sts.

Row 37: work in patt to marker, remove marker, sl1, k2tog, psso, remove marker, work in patt to end. 31 sts.

Right side of scarf

Work 5 rows in patt.

Row 6 (RS): work in patt to 5 sts from end, work buttonhole over 3 sts, p2. Work 11 rows in patt.

Row 18: work in patt to 5 sts from end, work buttonhole over 3 sts, p2. Rep last 12 rows once.
Work 5 rows in patt.

Row 36: sl1, k1, m1, work 13 sts in patt, m1, k1, m1, work 13 sts in patt, m1, k1, p1. 35 sts.
Work 1 row in patt.
Row 38: sl1, k1, m1, k1, work 13 sts in patt, (k1, m1) twice, k1, work 13 sts in patt, k1, m1, k1, p1. 39 sts.
Work 1 row in patt.
Row 40: sl1, (k1, m1p) twice, k1, work 13 sts in patt, k1, (m1p, k1) 4 times, work 13 sts in patt, k1, (m1p, k1) twice, p1. 47 sts. Work 3 rows in patt.
Row 44: sl1, (k1, m1p, p1) twice, ssk, work 11 sts in patt, k2tog, (m1p, p1, k1) 3 times, m1p, p1, ssk, work 11 sts in patt, k2tog, (m1p, p1, k1) twice, p1. 51 sts.
Work 1 row in patt.
Row 46: sl1, (k1, p2) twice, ssk, work 9 sts in patt, k2tog, (p2, k1) 3 times, p2, ssk, work 9 sts in patt, k2tog, (p2, k1) twice, p1. 47 sts.
Work 1 row in patt.
Row 48: sl1, (k1, p1, m1p, p1) twice, ssk, work 7 sts in patt, k2tog, (p1, m1p, p1, k1) 3 times, p1, m1p, p1, ssk, work 7 sts in patt, k2tog, (p1, m1p, p1, k1) twice, p1. 51 sts. Work 1 row in patt.

Row 50: sl1, (k1, p3) twice, ssk, work 5 sts in patt, k2tog, (p3, k1) 3 times, p3, ssk, work 5 sts in patt, k2tog, (p3, k1) twice, p1. 47 sts. Work 1 row in patt.
Row 52: sl1, (k1, p1, m1p, p2) twice, ssk, work 3 sts in patt, k2tog, (p1, m1p, p2, k1) 3 times, p1, m1p, p2, ssk, work 3 sts in patt, k2tog, (p1, m1p, p2, k1) twice, p1. 51 sts. Work 1 row in patt.
Row 54: sl1, (k1, p4) twice, ssk, p1, k2tog, (p4, k1) 3 times, p4, ssk, p1, k2tog, (p4, k1) twice, p1. 47 sts
Work 1 row in patt.
Row 56: sl1, (k1, p4) twice, k1, k2tog, (p4, k1) 3 times, p4, k1, k2tog, (p4, k1) twice, p1. 45 sts.
Work 2 rows in patt, bind off.

Finishing
Weave in ends. Sew buttons onto longer scarf section so that when the longer end is wrapped around the neck and the ends are crossed over the buttonholes line up with the buttons. Block flat, shaping ends into curves and opening up shells.

cast on

bind off

Scroll Lace Scarf

A pretty, lacey scarf that combines the work of two wonderfully talented friends of mine. Its shallow curved shape, perfect for gracefully wrapping around your neck, was inspired by Laura Chau's Just Enough Ruffles Scarf pattern and Lilith of Old Maiden Aunt created the beautiful yarn. The flowing, organic edging pattern, with its unusually large holes, is Victorian and although her identity is long lost I'm extremely grateful to the talented knitter who dreamed it up for me to use. All I can take credit for with this design is the mixing of all of these elements, but I love the result and hope you do too.

Originally published in Yarn Forward issue 15

Materials

246yds / 225m sportweight yarn. Shown in Old Maiden Aunt Alpaca / Silk Sportweight (80% alpaca / 20% silk, 3.53oz / 100g, 246yds / 255m) in Red red rose Size 9 US / 5.5mm 60cm or longer circular needle

Gauge

16 sts and 20 rows = 4" / 10cm in st st

Size

Approx 55" / 140cm long and 12" / 30cm wide

Directions

Scroll Lace Edging

Using a provisional method, cast on 12 sts.

Working from either written or charted instructions work rows 1-15, then repeat rows 2-15 until 28 repeats of scroll lace pattern has been worked.

Scarf Body

With WS facing, without breaking yarn and beginning next to last st worked, pick up and k 1 st for every 2 rows along straight side of edging. Turn. 208 sts.

Row 1 (RS): k124, w+t.

Row 2 (WS): p52, w+t.

Row 3: k to wrapped st, k wrap together with wrapped st, k5, w+t.

Row 4: p to wrapped st, p wrap together with wrapped st, p5, w+t.

Rows 5-10: rep rows 3-4 three more times.

Row 11: k to wrapped st, k wrap together with wrapped st, k3, w+t.

Row 12: p to wrapped st, p wrap together with wrapped st, p3, w+t.

Rows 13-32: rep rows 11-12 ten more times.

Row 33: k to wrapped st, k wrap together with wrapped st, k1, w+t.

Row 34: p to wrapped st, p wrap together with wrapped st, p1, w+t.

Row 35: k to wrapped st, k wrap together with wrapped st, k to end.

Row 36: k to wrapped st, k wrap together with wrapped st, k1; without turning undo provisional cast on and slip 12 held sts onto left needle tip; k across these 12 sts. 220 sts.

Picot Bind Off

Bind off 2 sts, *slip st on right needle back to left needle, cable cast on 2 sts, cast off 5 sts; rep from * until 2 sts rem, slip st on right needle back to left needle, cable cast on 2 sts, bind off rem sts.

Finishing

Weave in ends; block, pinning out points of edging and picot bind off and making sure the two ends are symmetrical.

Scroll Lace - Written Directions

Row 1: knit to last st, p1.

Row 2: sl1, k1, (yo, k2tog) twice, yo 4 times, k2tog twice, yo, k2.

Row 3: sl1, k to last st, working (k1, p1, k1, p1) into 4 yos from previous row, p1.

Row 4: sl1, k2, (yo, k2tog) twice, k4, k2tog, yo, k2.

Rows 5, 7, 9, 11 & 13: sl1, k to last st, p1.

Row 6: sl1, k3, (yo, k2tog) twice, k3, k2tog, yo, k2.

Row 8: sl1, k4, (yo, k2tog) twice, k2, k2tog, yo, k2.

Row 10: sl1, k5, (yo, k2tog) twice, k1, k2tog, yo, k2.

Row 12: sl1, k6, (yo, k2tog) twice, k2tog, yo, k2.

Row 14: sl1, k7, (yo, k2tog) twice, k3.

Row 15: bo3, k to last st, p1.

Scroll Lace - Chart

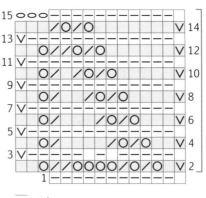

☐ k on rs, p on ws
– p on rs, k on ws
O yo
╱ k2tog on rs, ssk on ws
V sl1 pwise with yarn at wrong side

Cotton Reel Mittens

Fun, colourful mittens that can be made either fingerless or with closed tops to keep your fingers toasty warm. They combine traditional stranded colourwork techniques and shaping, with a simple and modern geometric pattern. The cuffs begin with an I-cord edging that creates little loops for hanging or for attaching an optional string, because even grown ups can lose their mittens and you put too much work into these for that! Colourful reels of cotton inspired my friend Natalie's wonderful dyeing. The colourwork pattern also echoes the shape of the ends of the reels, like the prints I made from them as a child.

Materials

Full version: 130yds / 118m, fingerless version: 100yds / 92m each of 2 colours of fingering weight (4ply) yarn.
Shown in Yarn Yard Clan(100% merino, 230 yds / 210m, 2.3oz /65g) in Botanic and Electric for full version and Happy and Doodle for fingerless version.
Size 3 US / 3.25 mm dpns.

Gauge

36 sts and 36 rnds = 4" / 10cm in stranded colourwork

Size

4" / 10cm across hand at widest point, full version are 9" / 23cm long and fingerless version are 7" / 18cm
Size can be changed by working at a slightly looser or tighter gauge.

Directions

I-cord edging

With 2 dpns and CC cast on 7 sts and work in I-cord: *k7, slide sts to other end of dpn without turning, rep from *; for 64 rows.

Bind off 4 sts. Continue working in I-cord on rem 3 sts for 12 more rows, bind off.

Picking up sts for mittens

Beg at cast on edge and working from right to left pick up and k 64 sts with CC along back of I-cord, pick up each st by picking up slightly loose strand between first and last sts and knitting into this loop as for a normal st.

Both mittens

Distribute sts evenly on dpns and join rnd; k 1 rnd in CC. Join MC and work from chart to marked row for fingerless mitts or all rows for full mittens.

Full Mittens

Using CC kitchener st rem sts together.

Fingerless mitts

Break CC, k 1 rnd in MC.
Work 6 rnds in k1, p1 rib. Bind off, for best results work a sewn tubular bind off or use another elastic method.

Thumbs

Return held thumb sts to needles; pick up and k sts across cast on sts as follows: 2 sts with MC, (1 with CC, 1 with MC) 4 times, 1 with CC, 2 with MC.

Distribute these 26 sts evenly over dpns and work row 1 of thumb chart. 24 sts.

Work row 2 of thumb chart 7 times for fingerless version and 17 times for full version.

For full version: work to end of thumb chart, break yarn and draw through rem sts, fastening tightly on inside.

For fingerless version:
Break CC, k 1 rnd in MC.
Work 6 rnds in k1, p1 rib. Bind off.

Finishing

Weave in ends, closing up any holes at base of thumbs and sewing ends of I-cord together so that the ends of the wider part are joined and the narrow part forms a loop. Block.

Optional: make a cord by twisting long lengths of the 2 colours together and doubling it back on itself. Fasten cord to I-cord loops so that mittens can hang at a comfortable length.

Whimsical Little Knits 2

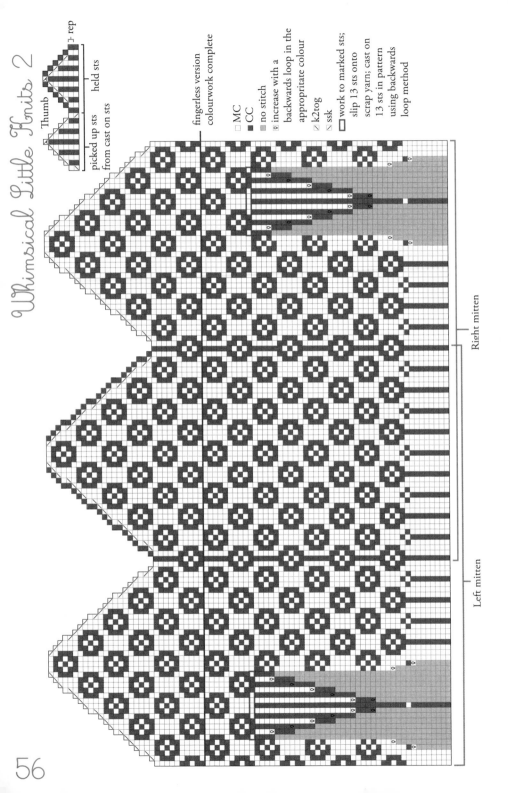

Thumb
held sts
picked up sts
from cast on sts
rep

fingerless version
colourwork complete

- □ MC
- ■ CC
- ▧ no stitch
- ⊙ increase with a backwards loop in the appropriate colour
- ▧ k2tog
- ⊠ ssk
- □ work to marked sts; slip 13 sts onto scrap yarn; cast on 13 sts in pattern using backwards loop method

Right mitten

Left mitten

For more patterns by Ysolda
visit www.ysolda.com